This collection of photographs has been selected carefully to represent the variety of sites to be seen and will help you to enjoy, again and again, the mysterious beauty of the Great Smoky Mountains National Park.

front cover: Great Smoky Mountains National Park from the Blue Ridge Parkway
right: Oliver Cabin, Cades Cove
following pages: Entrance to Cades Cove

great smoky mou

America's most popular National Park

tains

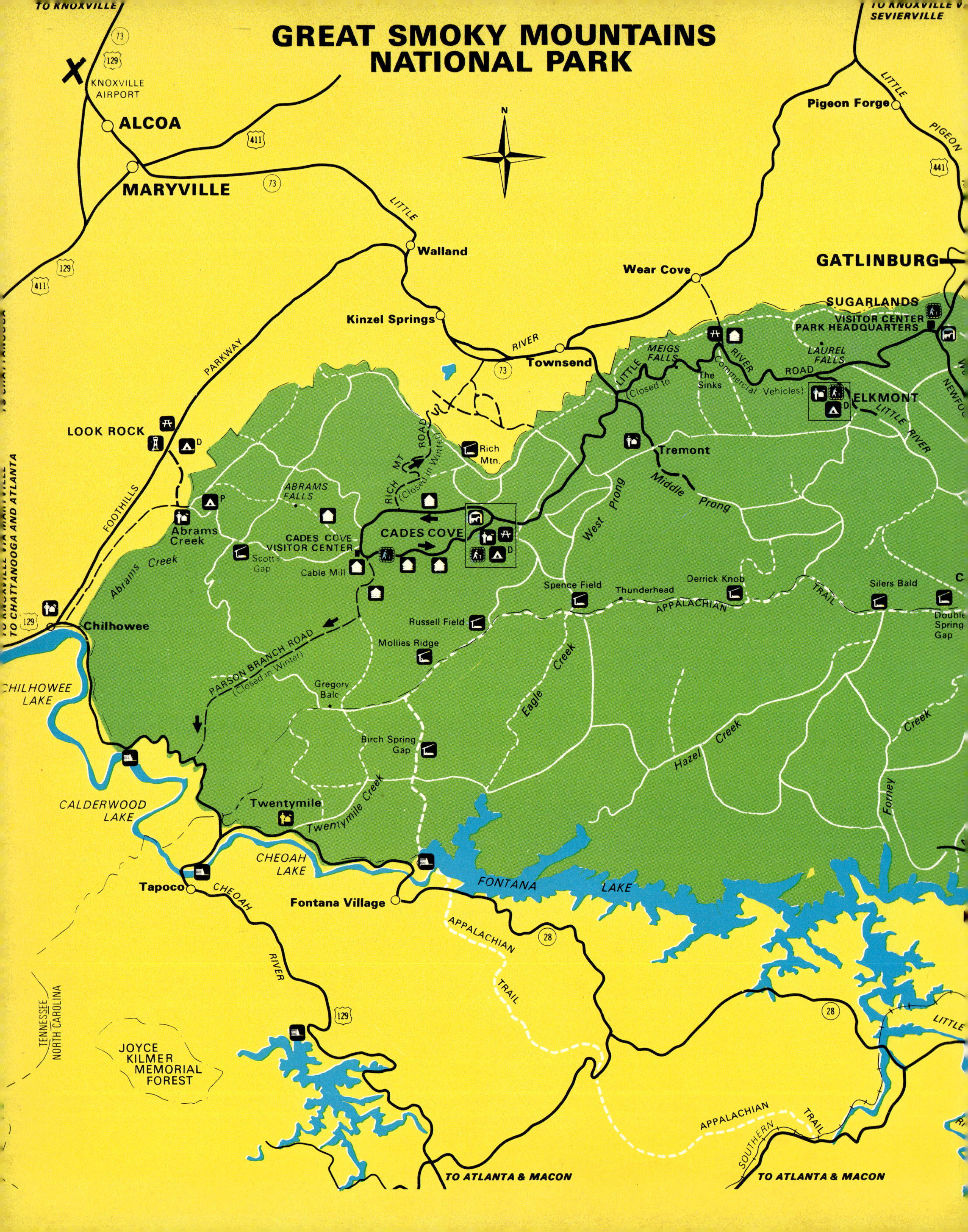

GREAT SMOKY MOUNTAINS
NATIONAL PARK
N
TO KNOXVILLE
TO KNOXVILLE V.
SEVIERVILLE
KNOXVILLE AIRPORT
ALCOA
MARYVILLE
Pigeon Forge
Walland
Wear Cove
GATLINBURG
Kinzel Springs
SUGARLANDS
VISITOR CENTER
PARK HEADQUARTERS
Townsend
MEIGS FALLS
LAUREL FALLS
LOOK ROCK
Rich Mtn.
The Sinks
Commercial Vehicles)
(Closed to
ELKMONT
LITTLE RIVER
Tremont
NEWFO
ABRAMS FALLS
RICH MT ROAD
(Closed in Winter)
Abrams Creek
CADES COVE VISITOR CENTER
CADES COVE
West Prong
Middle Prong
Scott's Gap
Cable Mill
Spence Field
Thunderhead
Derrick Knob
Silers Bald
C
Chilhowee
Russell Field
APPALACHIAN
TRAIL
Double Spring Gap
PARSON BRANCH ROAD
(Closed in Winter)
Mollies Ridge
Gregory Bald
Eagle Creek
Hazel Creek
Forney Creek
CHILHOWEE LAKE
Birch Spring Gap
CALDERWOOD LAKE
Twentymile
Twentymile Creek
FONTANA LAKE
CHEOAH LAKE
Tapoco
Fontana Village
FOOTHILLS PARKWAY
TO CHATTANOOGA
TO KNOXVILLE VIA MARYVILLE
TO CHATTANOOGA AND ATLANTA
CHEOAH RIVER
APPALACHIAN TRAIL
TENNESSEE
NORTH CAROLINA
JOYCE KILMER MEMORIAL FOREST
LITTLE RIVER
LITTLE RIVER ROAD
LITTLE PIGEON
TO ATLANTA & MACON
TO ATLANTA & MACON
APPALACHIAN TRAIL
SOUTHERN

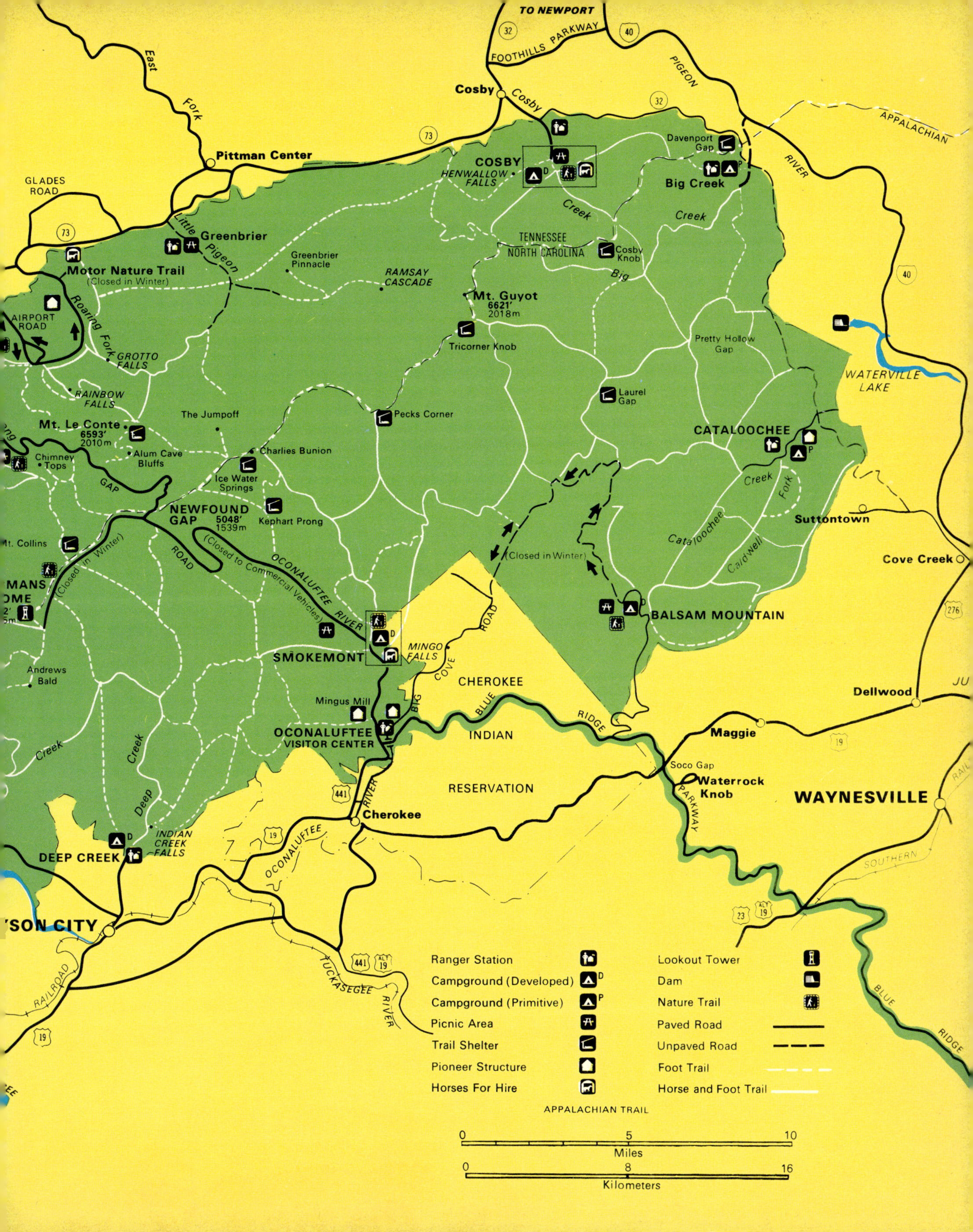
TO NEWPORT
32
FOOTHILLS PARKWAY
40
Cosby
Cosby
PIGEON
APPALACHIAN
Pittman Center
73
Davenport Gap
GLADES ROAD
COSBY
HENWALLOW FALLS
Big Creek
RIVER
40
73
Greenbrier
Motor Nature Trail
(Closed in Winter)
Little Pigeon
Greenbrier Pinnacle
RAMSAY CASCADE
TENNESSEE
NORTH CAROLINA
Creek
Cosby Knob
Creek
Big
AIRPORT ROAD
Roaring Fork
GROTTO FALLS
Mt. Guyot
6621'
2018m
Pretty Hollow Gap
RAINBOW FALLS
The Jumpoff
Tricorner Knob
WATERVILLE LAKE
Mt. Le Conte
6593'
2010m
Charlies Bunion
Pecks Corner
Laurel Gap
CATALOOCHEE
Chimney Tops
Alum Cave Bluffs
Ice Water Springs
GAP
Creek
Fork
Suttontown
NEWFOUND GAP
5048'
1539m
Kephart Prong
OCONALUFTEE RIVER
Cataloochee
Cardwell
Cove Creek
Mt. Collins
ROAD
(Closed to Commercial Vehicles)
(Closed in Winter)
276
CLINGMANS DOME
6642'
2025m
(Closed in Winter)
BALSAM MOUNTAIN
Andrews Bald
SMOKEMONT
MINGO FALLS
COVE
ROAD
CHEROKEE
Dellwood
JU
Mingus Mill
BLUE
INDIAN
Maggie
OCONALUFTEE VISITOR CENTER
Creek
Creek
RIDGE
Soco Gap
Waterrock Knob
WAYNESVILLE
Deep
441
RESERVATION
PARKWAY
DEEP CREEK
INDIAN CREEK FALLS
RIVER
Cherokee
SOUTHERN
RAIL
BRYSON CITY
19
OCONALUFTEE
441
23
ACT
19
RAILROAD
TUCKASEGEE
RIVER
19
441
ACT
19
BLUE
RIDGE
Ranger Station
Lookout Tower
Campground (Developed)   D
Dam
Campground (Primitive)   P
Nature Trail
Picnic Area
Paved Road
Trail Shelter
Unpaved Road
Pioneer Structure
Foot Trail
Horses For Hire
Horse and Foot Trail
APPALACHIAN TRAIL
0   5   10
Miles
0   8   16
Kilometers

Great Smoky Mountains National Park

The most popular National Park in America is a territory of 800 square miles, about 60 miles in length and 20 miles in width that straddles the west border of North Carolina and the east border of Tennessee. It is a magnificent location of Vacation Land for the crowded East of our Nation.

Geologists tell us that over two hundred million years ago, there was a great upheaval of the Earth's surface in this Appalachian area and the Great Smoky Mountains were formed from a shallow sea. For these millions of years, erosion of water and wind did its work. Valleys and slopes which exist today were formed — and now we have 16 peaks over 6,000 feet and 53 over 5,000 feet in height. The valleys range from a low point of 857 feet at Abrams Creek on the west and ascends in a broken array of valleys and peaks to a height of 6,642 feet at Clingmans Dome, the highest mountain in the park. All this forms a panorama of beauty. Within its borders you will find deep gorges, gentle slopes, rapid streams, clear pools, jagged rocks, great forests and rich meadows.

Plant life is in profusion. You will find 1,300 kinds of flowering shrubs and plants, 130 different kinds of trees, nearly 30 varieties of orchids and grasses of all kinds. Nourished by a rich soil, a heavy rainfall (about 80 inches), and the sun of our most temperate zone makes the area of this Park one of the most luxuriant of the World — the Kashmir, the Shangri-La of America.

The profuse growth of vegetation (being close packed Rhododendron and Mountain Laurel) combines with the oil of the pines to exude an aroma and a vapor that rises and mixes with the feathery fleece of the fog. It clings to the top of the mountains and sinks to the valleys below — and you have the Smokies, and the reason for the name — The Great Smoky Mountains National Park.

Let us tell you how the Smokies became one of our National Parks. As you may know, most all of our other parks were set aside from government lands and before the private individual could claim any ownership. However, with the Smokies it was different. For years its land was owned by private individuals and lumber companies as it contained one of the finest spreads of lumber in the United States. Spruce, fir and hemlock — oak, walnut and other fine woods grew straight and tall. Then came the devastating forces of man. Private enterprise in the form of saw mills began to destroy one of the most beautiful wilderness areas of the nation.

Fortunately, one of the reasons we are a great nation and people is that in time of need there always has been an individual who has come to our rescue. In this case, Mrs. Willis P. Davis of Knoxville, Tennessee, who realized the grandeur of the area, started a movement to change the entire complex to a National Park.

Others followed — and John D. Rockefeller, Jr. contributed $ 5,000,000. This amount was added to funds from State, Federal and private sources and the lands of the Smokies was purchased and given to the Federal Government. On September 8, 1940, the Great Smoky Mountains National Park became a reality when it was formally dedicated by President Franklin D. Roosevelt.

by John Locke

following pages: Gatlinburg, Tennessee at the entrance to the Great Smoky Mountains National Park.

Gatlinburg, Tennessee
top left: The Sky Lift
top right: Looking south towards
Mt. Le Conte
right: Looking east from the By-pass

The entrance to the Great Smoky Mountains
National Park near Gatlinburg

GREAT SMOKY
MOUNTAINS
NATIONAL PARK
UNITED STATES DEPARTMENT OF THE INTERIOR
NATIONAL PARK SERVICE

top: Visitor Center Park Headquarters
at Sugarlands
right: Little River at the entrance to the Park

right: Le Conte Lodge, available only on foot, and Mt. Le Conte

Mt. Mitchell 6684' (2037 m)
Mt. Le Conte 6593' (2010 m)

top left: Alun Cave Bluffs;
top right: Charlies Bunion;
botton left: Rainbow Falls;
botton right: The Old Mill on background;
right: Grotto Falls.

The Appalachian Trail enters the Park at Fontana and Davenport Gap, crossing about 88 miles of the Great Smoky Mountains National Park.

top left: Sunset near Charlies Bunion;
top righ: Heath Balds in the southwest section of the park;
bottom left: one of the bear-proof trail shelters;
bottom right: a trail marker.

left: The Chimney Tops along the Little
Pigeon River
above: Ramsay Cascade

following pages: A magnificent sunset
from Clingmans Dome

Clingmans Dome 6642' (2025 m), the highest mountain in the Park

top: A sunset seen from the roadway at Newfound Gap,
bottom: The parking area at Newfound Gap and a glimpse of Highway 441 winding its way through the Park.
at left: The crisp white lovliness of a winter snow adds a special magic to Newfound Gap 5048' (1539 m)

following pages: south of Newfound Gap on the Skyway, looking to the west

Kanati Fork on the Oconaluftee River

top: Scenic U.S. 441 forms this exciting loop as it climbs from Gatlinburg to 5048' (1539 m) at Newfound Gap,
bottom: an overlook along Transmountain Highway 441 shows one of the multitude of breathtaking views discovered at virtually every bend

In springtime, the Park returns to new life and is resplendent with dogwood blooms from middle to late April.

The roadways in the Park take on a special brilliance in autumn, a favorite time for visitors. **left:** The Great Smoky Mountains National Park seen from the Blue Ridge Parkway near Cherokee, North Carolina.

top: Coming down the Skyway toward Cherokee,
North Carolina,
bottom: Mingus Mill near Cherokee

Indian Creek Falls near Bryson City

Aunt Winchester, matriarch of the Smokies.
This painting of the resident of the Great
Smoky Mountains at the age of 100 years
is hanging in the Oconaluftee Visitor
Center.

At the southern entrance to the Great
Smoky Mountains National Park,
this Ranger Station and Pioneer Museum
displays pioneer artifacts covering nearly
two centuries of life in the Southern
Highlands.

At the entrance to the Great Smoky
Mountains National Park near Cherokee,
North Carolina.

below: The Blue Ridge Parkway joining U.S.
441 near the Oconaluftee Visitor Center

The Qualla Cherokee Indian Reservation
joins the Great Smoky Mountains National
Park at the southern entrance.
It is the home of the Eastern band of the
Cherokee Indians, many of whom were forced
to Oklahoma on the infamous
"Trail of Tears" march.

The Oconaluftee Indian Village depicts
the Cherokee way of life where you can see
an interesting study of the past, as well as see
the handwork and crafts of the Cherokee.

left: The Park often reveals an interesting
display of Nature at work. top: Mingo Falls

following pages: Hazel Creek overlooking
Fontana Lake

top: A view of the Smokies from
Fontana Village,
bottom, thirty-mile Fontana Lake and Dam
provides a natural boundary along the southern
end of the Park and is the highest Dam in the
East, 480 feet high.

Fontana Village

Sight along the Little River Road between
Sugarlands and Cades Cove, a dynamic series
of cascades and rapids; top left: Laurel Falls;
and top right: the "Great Stone Face".

Abrams Falls

The foot trail on the way
to Abrams Falls offers many
surprises for those who take
the time to look.

Cades Cove

Parsons Branch Road

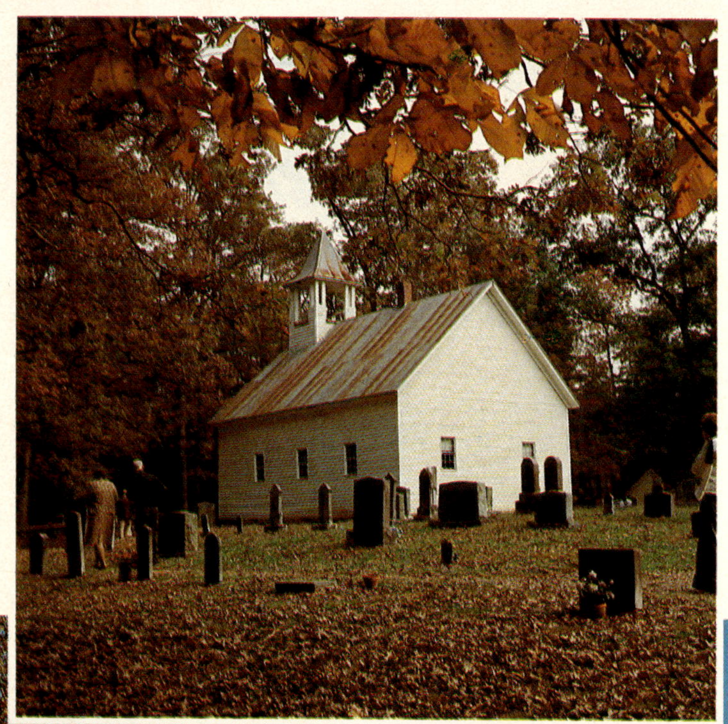

Cades Cove Primitive
Baptist Church

The Peter Cable House

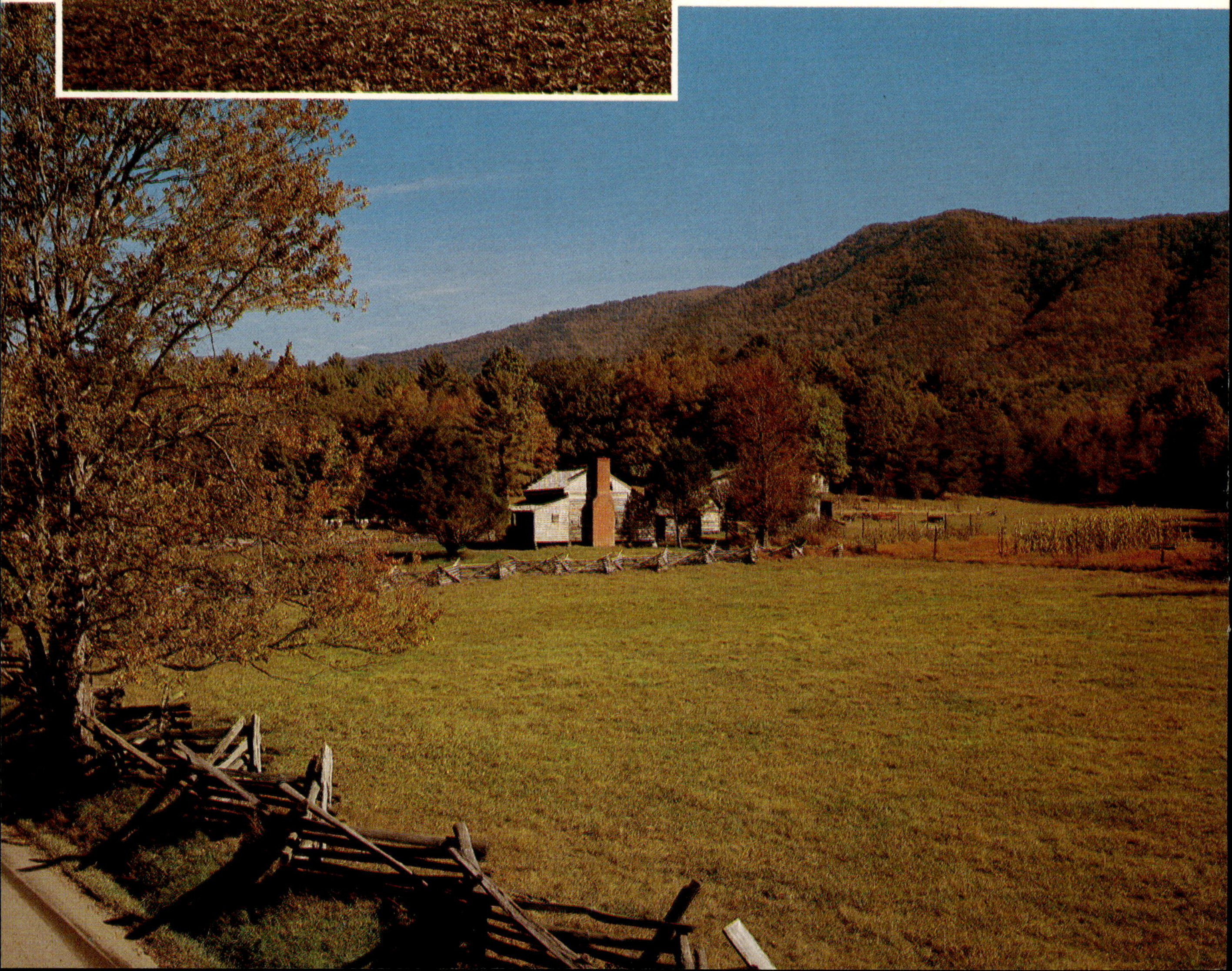

top left: Palmer's Chapel Methodist Church,
top right: Henry Whitehead Place,
bottom left: Elijah Oliver Place,
bottom right: Program Shelter and
Campground Store

The Becky Cable House may have
been the first frame house
in the Cove.
At left, the John Cable Mill and Wade
Effler, an old-time miller,
demonstrates actual production
of corn meal at the only grist mill
left in the Park which uses
an overshoot wheel.

The sorghum mill was powered
by horse or mule to squeeze
the juice from sorghum canes.
At left, the Visitor Center
at Cable Mill and Becky
Cable House.

In early Spring pink-bud, dowwood and mountain laurel lend delicate tints of color to the new greens of leafing trees.

Signaling the end of a beautiful day, this tranquil setting
reflects the sun on the eleven mile Loop Road and depicts
the peace and serenity of this little bit of Heaven.
Cades Cove in the Great Smoky Mountains National Park.